YOU

You Can Be The Difference

Breaking the cycle of being a bully, victim or bystander

Barbara Chandler, B.Msc

You Can Be The Difference

Copyright © 2020 by Barbara Chandler, B.Msc

All rights reserved.

No part of this book may be reproduced or utilized in any form or by any means, electronic or mechanical, including photocopying, recording or by any information storage and retrieval system without the permission in writing from the author.

Carlene Sears – Editor and Copywriter

Jessica Renko – Editor and Education

Vitek Graphic Designs – Cover design

Laura Baker – Cover photographer

ISBN: 9798612013594

Email: youcanbethedifference@comcast.net

YOU CAN BE THE DIFFERENCE

*Be the person who breaks
the cycle.
If you were judged,
choose understanding.
If you were rejected,
choose acceptance.
If you were shamed,
choose compassion.
Be the person you needed when
you were hurting, not the person
who hurt you.
Vow to be better than what
broke you – to heal
instead of becoming bitter,
so you can act from your heart
and not your pain.*

Lori Dechene

YOU CAN BE THE DIFFERENCE

Dedication

In memory of:
Jason Matthew Chandler
September 30, 1982 – August 19, 2013

This book is dedicated to my late son, Jason, who was bullied in junior high school so badly he started to do drugs to ease the pain. His drug use continued throughout high school and his life until August 19, 2013. Jason was 30 when he died from an accidental cocaine overdose.

I will never see his contagious smile, hear his silly laugh, listen to his stories, or have him home for the holidays again. If I want to be with Jason, I have to visit him at the cemetery.

This book is for all the bullied victims and their families who endure this nightmare on a daily basis.

This book is for all the families who have lost a child or someone they love by suicide because of bullying.

I hope this book provides you with the information you need to understand how your words and actions impact those around you. We all have the power to make powerful contributions to society, be good friends, impact the world in a positive way and make good choices for ourselves and those around us. My prayer is that this book will help you think about your choices more carefully and make the choice that will result in the most positive consequences for yourself and those around you.

YOU CAN BE THE DIFFERENCE

CONTENTS

Acknowledgements

1	Bullying: A growing problem	1
2	Bullies	4
3	Cyberbullying	22
4	Victims	31
5	Bystanders	38
6	I pledge to be an Upstander	43
7	Make a Difference	45
8	Resources	48
9	Need Some Inspiration?	50
10	Activity	53
	About the Author	55
	References	59

YOU CAN BE THE DIFFERENCE

Acknowledgements

I want to thank my wonderful inspiring daughter, Jessica, for the initial edit and all the support and encouragement you have given me throughout the years living with Jason. You are my rock!

A very special thank-you to Valery Green, my best friend, for being there for me when Jason was growing up. Having you there to vent to, cry to, seek for advice, or just hold my hand. You are a true friend who has given me so much support during the trying times.

And a very special thank-you to Adrienne White, my best friend, who always had encouraging words through all the trying times after losing my husband and during the times with Jason. She is also familiar with family addiction which is where I needed the support the most.

To Carlene Sears, for editing my book and making sure that it is appropriate for junior high and high school students. And for all the research you put into it to make it the best informative book. You turned my vision into a reality, thank you.

To Laura Baker Photography for the cover and back photo for the book. You helped me with my vision.

To Vitek Designs for designing the front cover. You turned my vision into a powerful cover.

To all the resources that gave me permission to reprint their stories to help people understand the lasting effects on bullying.

1

Bullying: A growing problem

This morning when I turned on the news, there was another story of an 11-year-old girl that hanged herself after being bullied. Her peers bullied her for changing her hairstyle. The bullies told her to go and kill herself and she did. Terrifyingly, this little girl is just one of the many thousands who succumb to the pressures of being bullied.

What do you think she thought about right before she killed herself? Was she crying for her mother to hold her? Was she crying for a solution to stop the bullying? Did she feel alone? Did she feel that ending her life was her only solution?

How many of you have 11-year-old siblings, cousins or friends? How would your family feel if this happened to them?

Families of victims are devastated and struggle to understand their loved one's decision to commit suicide. They'll never see another birthday, graduation, wedding, or other future accomplishment of their child, grandchild, sibling, or cousin. All because someone felt it was ok to cross a boundary and say something hurtful. This old adage is a good one to follow to ensure you are mindful of others' feelings: If you can't say anything nice, don't say anything at all.

Bullying by the Numbers
Do Something, a 2.5 million member organization that focused on young people and changing the social scene for today's youth, estimates that more than 1 out of every 5 students age 12-18 faces bullying during the school year. Fifty-seven percent of bullying situations stop when a peer intervenes on behalf of the student being bullied.[i]

Studies done by Yale University indicate that victims of bullying are between 2 and 9 times more likely to consider suicide than non-victims.[ii] While there are many reasons why people consider and attempt suicide, it's important for each of us to make sure we are treating others kindly and with respect to help them feel like they belong. This simple act could go a long way in helping lower the rate of students considering and/or attempting suicide, as you'll read about in A Story About a Boy Named Kyle later in this book.

Is your school doing enough to educate or reprimand students when it comes to bullying? Would you want to hear about another child who was bullied so badly they thought the only way to make it stop was to end their life? There are too many victims suffering in silence and afraid to speak up. A victim could be sitting right next to you and you might not even know it!

Encouragement

It doesn't have to be this way. Everyone's life is so important! Everyone has value, a purpose to be the best that they can be. Each person deserves the chance to show the world that they are powerful people who can make a difference.

This book will empower you to make sure that no one else suffers at the hands of a bully.

2

Bullies

"Words can break someone into a million pieces, but they can also put them back together. I hope you use yours for good, because the only words you'll regret more than the ones left unsaid are the ones you use to intentionally hurt someone."
Taylor Swift

Read
A brain cancer survivor commits suicide because bullies were making fun of her looks. Bethany had brain cancer eight years ago and after having a tumor removed was left with a crooked smile. Bethany, 11, got off the bus, went onto her porch and shot herself.[iii]

Reflect
As you are reading the examples of bullying behavior in this book, take some time to reflect:
- Is this me?
- Do I intentionally make life seem impossible for someone?
- Am I laughing at people who are different than me?
- Do I put people down to make myself feel good?

- Do I think it's funny to gang up on someone?
- Do I feel satisfied when I call someone names?
- Do I think it's okay to destroy someone's property?
- Do I feel sad or upset when I see someone hurt?
- Do I get pleasure from torturing animals?

Forty-two percent of students who reported being bullied at school said their bullying was related to a characteristic like their appearance, race, gender, disability, ethnicity, religion or sexual orientation.[iv] Think about your own biases and how you might see someone. Do you look at someone and only see their exterior characteristics like those listed above?

Encouragement
If you answered yes to any of these questions, this book will turn your thinking around. This book will help you see a person no different from yourself when you look at another.

There are better, more constructive questions you can ask that will help you make sure your peers, friends, family members and even strangers feel that they belong. Here are some questions:
- Can I tell if someone needs help?
- Do I offer to help when someone needs it?

- Do I stand up for people who are bullied?
- Do I show sympathy when someone is down?
- Do I offer a shoulder to someone who is crying?
- Do I support my friends?

If you answered yes to these questions, then you will create lifelong friendships and contribute to a better world. You show love and compassion to others and are a selfless person. You are more of what this world needs!

In the chapter about Victims, there are questions you can use to help determine if you or someone you know is a victim of bullying. There are resources at the end of this book to help you or your peer report the bullying and/or cope with it in a healthy way.

Learn
Bullying can take on many different forms. Many people may not even consider their actions bullying until they stop and think about how their "fun" and "teasing" could really impact someone.

1) **CYBERBULLYING.** Cyberbullying is a growing trend and involves verbal aggression (threatening or harassing) and relational aggression (spreading rumors) online.[v] Messages spread quickly via the Internet, and do not go away, even if they are deleted by the

user. Many times, other users take screenshots of bullying and repost them, making it impossible to know whether a hurtful message has ever truly been eliminated even if it was deleted. The victim of cyberbullying can either see the hurtful message or hear about it. The victim can begin to believe the message or feel alone and isolated because of the message, which can cause depression or other emotional health issues[vi] and can even contribute to suicidal thoughts or attempts.

Cyberbullying occurs on social media platforms, such as Facebook, Instagram, Snapchat, Twitter, TikTok, YouTube, Ask.fm, and more.

   a. **SEXTING.** Sexting is sending a sexually explicit message or image using a cell phone.[vii] When a bully gets hold of an embarrassing or inappropriate picture of someone, they can share it widely via social media. This can be humiliating for the victim and could lead to in-person and cyberbullying by people they know and do not know.

2) **PHYSICAL BULLYING.** Physical bullying includes hitting, punching, shoving, or other acts meant to intentionally cause physical harm to someone.[viii]

3) **VERBAL BULLYING.** Name calling,

teasing, and using words to harm another person are all forms of verbal bullying.[ix]

Some children in junior high school can be more vulnerable to becoming bullies because their parents may not have taken the time to teach them right from wrong, they suffered a trauma, or they have a deep desire to feel accepted because they have low self-esteem.[x] Some children have bullies for parents and are the victims themselves, so that's all they know.

Encouragement
No matter what your parents did or did not do or what you might have experienced in your life, YOU have the power to be a good person. When I was growing up, both of my parents were alcoholics and my mother was a verbally and emotionally abusive hypochondriac. I didn't let that stop me from becoming the caring, loving, fun person I am today. I have compassion for people and I will do everything in my power to make sure no one suffers at the hands of a bully.

You get to choose your surroundings. You get to choose who you want to be and hang around with. You have the opportunity to make your legacy. Do you want to be remembered as someone who was always there to help? Or do you want to be remembered as someone who hurt others?

Most bullies will forget about their victims years

down the road, but the victims may never forget who bullied them. And the impact of the bully's words can stay with the victim into adulthood.[xi]

Read
Here is a story from a victim where the bully apologized years later.
Reprinted with permission from The Bully Project. Names have been changed upon request.

Hi,

When I was younger in the 6th-8th grade in 2003-2004 (currently 23) I was a victim of bullying and of physical abuse by kids at my middle school for coming out as a lesbian and for being overweight... I had 4 major bullies in middle school and they caused me nothing but hell and grief to the point I wanted to commit suicide.... Yesterday out of the blue 1 of the 4 bullies came forward and gave me a heartfelt apology for how she treated me in middle school...... I would really like to share this story with kids and to show them that even years later some bullies do apologize and it does give closure to those they bullied.... Her name is Mindy (name changed).

Mindy: *Hey Lisa from time to time I remember being mean/bullying to you in middle school. I want to tell you how sorry I am for that and how much I regret doing so to this day. I was a dumb kid trying to fit in at the expense of others and I just want you to know it deeply bothers me to* *this day that I did so. I am so sorry if I ever caused any pain you are a beautiful strong person and deserve the best just like anybody else.....*

<u>Me:</u> *Why did you tell me this now?? After so many years.... Are you telling me this now as another joke or to poke fun at me for believing you??? You, and 3 others where my worst tormentors in school, you all made me want to kill myself (which is why I moved away after middle school)..... You all treated me bad just because I came out as gay, and that I was overweight.... I don't understand why u tell me now....*

<u>Mindy:</u> *No I truly mean it I was hurting on the inside myself. I'm so sorry for the pain I caused. I was angry as a child it took me YEARS to get over this anger and to find myself I hated myself when I was younger I was just taking it out on you. I am so sorry Lisa I can't take back what I did but I can at least tell you how much I regret it and how much it will always bother me about myself, it is what I deserve. You have been in my subconscious for a very long time I don't know why I didn't say something before maybe because I was too coward too or because of the shame I felt for treating you like that. I was watching a documentary on bullying and it literally brought tears to my eyes how these kids were being treated and what happened because of it. I thought of you again and figured it would* *only be right for you to know that I recognize what I did and I am not proud of it.*

Me: *Well thank you very much for coming forward.... At least 1 of 4 has.... And the documentary is called BULLY.... We showed it here in my town to everyone and to all the schools.... I and several others talked about our childhood and being bullied.... Thank you for some closure though...*

Mindy: *Your welcome I wish I would have done it sooner I was just a stupid kid trying to fit in none of it was ever true about you.*[xii]

Reflect
How many of you find yourself craving acceptance when you are with your friends? You see them doing something stupid, and you go along with it because you don't want to be called a sissy, coward, or chicken. Will you cave into bullying someone, taking drugs, vaping or drinking just to fit in?

True friends are beneficial to your health and would never encourage you to do something that would harm you or cause you to harm someone else. They will increase your sense of belonging and purpose and boost your happiness while also supporting you through difficult times in life.[xiii] The ones who challenge you to do things you don't want to do are bullying you.

It is not okay to belittle someone. It is not okay to embarrass someone. It is not okay to call someone names. It is not okay to harass someone. It is not okay to physically assault someone. It is NOT okay to make someone feel so bad that they want to end their lives to end the pain of being bullied.

If you wake up knowing you are going to use words to hurt someone, think again.
If you wake up knowing you are going to fight someone, think again.
If you wake up knowing you are going to spread rumors about someone, think again.
If you wake up knowing you are going to try and publicly embarrass someone, think again.

You have no right to make fun of or hurt anyone. You have no right to push them down, laugh at them, hurt them, or destroy their self-esteem. You have no right to gossip about anyone or try to embarrass them. And no one has the right to do this to you.

"Belittling others make you neither tough nor impressive. It makes you look stupid and rude."
Author Unknown

Take a good look in the mirror. What do you see? Do you see someone who feels empowered or good when you treat someone badly? If you do, please seek help. Deep down, you are better than that and you need someone to show you how to be that person that is crying to come out. If you are bullying, it is because you are hurting so much inside that you want others to hurt as much as you do.

There are many people who can and will help you, if you take the first step to ask. Go to an adult that you trust. See your school counselor, talk with your social worker, talk to your priest, rabbi, or a close friend you can trust to help you. There are many support groups online where you can feel safe sharing your stories.

I once heard someone say this on a talk show, and it made me pause and reflect: "If there is ever a time when you are looking at someone and there is something about them you don't like, they are not the one with the problem. You are."

Encouragement
There is a simple way to help make sure your words will build someone up rather than tear them down. Think about what you are doing and think about how it will affect someone. THINK before you speak:

Is it *True*?
Is it *Helpful*?
Is it *Inspiring*?
Is it *Necessary*?
Is it *Kind*?

Your words are powerful. If it makes you feel important or powerful to put someone else down, then you need to ask yourself why. Why am I doing this? Why do I enjoy making people feel less than me? Why do I like hurting people? Is it because I've been hurt myself? Is it because I am looking for attention? Is it because I believe people will think I am cool if I do?

"People who love themselves, don't hurt other people. The more we hate ourselves, the more we want others to suffer."
Dan Pearce

Learn
Research shows that being bullied can cause lasting damage to the victims. And physical bullying isn't the only type that causes lasting harm. Words, gestures, rumors and even intentionally not including someone can cause long-term damage to the victim. Victims of bullying suffer damage to their self-esteem and identities, which can damage a person's ability to view themselves as desirable, capable, loved and important.[xiv]

When a child is bullied, it not only effects the victim, it effects the whole family. Parents and siblings can feel powerless and as if they are failing to protect their child, brother or sister.[xv]

Kids who bully others are more likely to abuse

alcohol and other drugs, get into fights, drop out of school and have criminal convictions.[xvi]

Reflect

*"I believe we can all come together, because if you take away the labels, you realize, we're far more alike than different.
Ellen DeGeneres*

The girl you just called fat may have a medical condition and her medication makes her gain weight.
The boy you just called stupid may have a learning disability and works hard by studying long hours to keep up with the class.
The girl you just called ugly may spend hours putting on makeup to help her feel prettier.
The boy you just tripped may experience abuse at home and consider school his only safe place.
That guy you just made fun of for crying may be experiencing a trauma at home, such as a sick or dying parent.
That girl you just made fun of for being bald may have undergone chemotherapy for cancer treatment.
The boy you called poor may have to work every night to help support his family.
The old man you made fun of because of his ugly scars may have fought for our country.

Unless you have walked in their shoes, don't

assume you know them.

Encouragement
If you see someone struggling to make friends or being bullied, you have the opportunity to make a positive impact on them. Say hi or at least smile at them in the hallway. You never know what that person might be facing outside of school. Your kindness might just be the BIG difference in their life.

If you see a kid sitting alone at school, go and sit with them. Get to know them. They just might be your new best friend!

There are some wonderful stories out there that demonstrate kindness over bullying:

A Michigan High School football team allowed the team water boy, who has special needs, to score a touchdown to surprise his terminally ill mom.[xvii]

At Olivet School in Olivet, Michigan, the middle school football team secretly devised a plan to let a young man with special needs score a touchdown. This act helped the team quarterback, who admitted that he thought he was cool and popular and only thought about himself, see the value and importance of helping someone else achieve something so great. This simple act of kindness changed the quarterback's life and helped a boy with special needs do something he will remember forever.[xviii]

If you are a bully, you can change and make a difference. Be the person that people look up to. Be the person that people want to be around. Be the person that others will remember for doing good. Stop hanging around kids that are constantly doing harmful things.

Read
One Teen was Bullied to Suicide. A Bullying Story, From The Bully[xix]
Reprinted with permission from Your Teen Mag.

By Kirk Zajac

What makes a person influential? Is it their actions, their friendship, their life? For me, Andrei Philip Lehman didn't influence me through his life, but unfortunately, through his death.

Andrei, known as Andy, was a senior at Notre Dame Cathedral Latin when I was a sophomore. Andy was a genius, effortlessly completing the most advanced courses in high school. Described by his father as "a true renaissance man," Andy was especially brilliant in mathematics, able to compute complex equations in his head. A winner of the National Merit Scholarship, Andy was granted early acceptance to many prestigious colleges.

But my classmates and I saw Andy as too smart to have social value. We saw him as a geek and an easy target. We wondered aloud why he still rode the school bus as a senior. We taunted him about his weight, calling him "polar bear." Because that moniker stuck, we never even knew his real name.

For most of the year, I was the ringleader of this horrible circus. I bullied him constantly.

September 19, 2006, began as a typical day. I took my seat with the rest of my business class and noticed that the usually punctual Mrs. McNulty was late. When she finally arrived, she was crying. As the students exchanged looks of wonder, morning announcements came over the loudspeaker. Principal Waler instructed us to pay close attention to an important announcement: Andy Lehman had passed away.

Silence filled the room as I wondered to myself, "Who was Andy Lehman?" The name was familiar, but I couldn't conjure up a face. Students pouring into the halls exchanged nervous looks; some crying, some, like me, staring blankly into the distance. A close friend of mine, Colleen Heffner, ran up to me. Mascara and eyeliner ran down her face as she cried and embraced me. She could only manage a few words: "It's Polar Bear."

During second period, Mr. Waler addressed the student body.

With great pain and sadness, he explained that "Last night, at 8:38 p.m., Andy Lehman died by suicide."

I don't remember much after that, as a tingling feeling of guilty shame ran up my spine and through my arms and sweaty hands. I felt solely responsible and guilty for Andy's death—he was bullied to suicide. Mr. Waler continued to speak as I sat frozen at my desk, unable to move or look anyone else in the eye. That moment will replay in my mind forever.

Three months after Andy's death, I shuffled downstairs and stepped into the kitchen to eat breakfast. Glancing at the News-Herald, a headline caught my eye: "Dad Pushes for Depression Awareness." The article began: "On Sept. 18, one of the area's brightest teenagers took his own life without warning. Now, three months after that tragic event, his father is trying to piece together what went wrong and looking for ways to help prevent such tragedies from occurring again."

In that instant, I knew that I needed to pay my respects to the man who lost his only son to suicide.

I needed to tell my responsibility in bullying his son. Sadly, had I not seen that article, I might never have realized that I needed to make things right.

That night, I walked one street north from my house to Mr. Lehman's house. I had no pre-

written apology, no mental notes of what to say to a grieving father. I didn't know what to expect, but I hoped that some piece of my guilt might be wiped away.

Five minutes later, I sat in the Lehmans' kitchen, and told the story that had been bottled up inside of me. Three hours later, I had learned so much about Andy. He and I had similarities; we had both seriously considered suicide and both suffered from teenage depression. I learned that while many factors contributed to his suicide, our bullying, combined with his deep depression, undeniably led him to act.

I couldn't absorb everything that night; it took days to sink in. Mr. Lehman had welcomed me into his home and appreciated my sharing a larger piece of the puzzle of his son's life. There was no anger on his part—only love.

Since that day, my mission has been preventing tragedies like Andy's.

I have the honor of working with Mr. Lehman and the Suicide Prevention Education Alliance, as a certified speaker and teacher of their core curriculum throughout the Cleveland area. I strive to fulfill this mission as well as I can, for Andy's sake.

The biggest lesson I learned from Andy is that our words always matter, and they can hurt more than physical pain. I knew nothing about Andy, and I had neither the common courtesy to care, nor the compassion to stop taunting him. I will live with that burden for the rest of my life. When Andy died, he became a part of me, ingrained in my soul forever. His legacy lives on through me, as I work to prevent teen suicide.

R.I.P. Andy Lehman

YOU CAN BE THE DIFFERENCE

3

Cyberbullying

The beautiful souls that left too early for no reason except for the relentless bullying.

Read
The following stories show the impact cyberbullying can have on a person.

Story retold with permission from the Tyler Clementi Foundation.

Tyler Clementi was an 18-year-old university freshman who loved playing the violin. Tyler committed suicide after he had a sexual encounter with a man in his dorm room that was allegedly video streamed over the internet, without Tyler's knowledge, by his roommate.[xx]

The following stories are retold with permission from Puresight.com.

Hannah Smith was a 14-year-old from Lutterworth, Leicestershire, England. Hannah's sister found her body in her bedroom in August 2013.

Bullies taunted Hannah about her weight and a family death on Ask.fm, an anonymous question-and-answer social networking site. Hannah's bullies told her she should drink bleach and cut herself.

After Hannah died, her father found a note from her that said: "As I sit here day by day I wonder if it's going to get better. I want to die, I want to be free. I can't live like this any more I'm not happy."

Hannah's older sister began to receive abusive messages on Facebook mocking Hannah's death and blaming their father for Hannah's suicide.[xxi]

Phoebe Prince was a 15-year-old student at South Hadley High School in Massachusetts. Phoebe killed herself just two days before her school's winter dance. Phoebe was new to the school and a victim of cyberbullying. Her peers were bullying her about her date for the dance, a senior football player.

Phoebe's bullies used Twitter, Craigslist, Facebook, and Formspring, and also verbally abused her in person at school. She was called "Irish slut" and "whore." After Phoebe's death, girls continued to bully Phoebe by posting messages on the Facebook page created in her memory. [xxii]

Phoebe's bullies were sentenced on harassment charges. In her public apology and statement to the judge, one of Phoebe's bullies cried, saying, "Phoebe…I'm sorry. I'm sorry for the unkind words I said about you. I'm sorry for what I wrote on my Facebook page. Most of all, I'm sorry for Jan. 14, in the library and in the hallway, when I laughed when someone was shouting humiliating things about you. I am immensely ashamed of myself."[xxiii]

David Molak was a sophomore at a Texas high school. David loved working out, the Spurs and being an Eagle Scout. David committed suicide in his family's backyard in January 2016 after being the target of ongoing bullying at school. His peers would send him text messages putting him down and insulting him. His 24-year-old brother, Cliff Molak, posted this online after David's suicide: "In today's age, bullies don't push you into lockers, they don't tell their victims to meet them behind the school's dumpster after class. They cower behind usernames and fake profiles from miles away constantly berating and abusing good, innocent people."[xxiv]

The following stories have been retold with permission from Lead Them Home. Loving LGBT+ People in the Church.

Kenneth Weishuhn Jr. was a 14-year-old when he came out as gay and some of his friends began to bully him. People he thought of as friends sent him death threats and started a Facebook group meant to spread hate against Kenneth. Kayla, Kenneth's sister, said she saw people Kenneth considered friends turn on him and bully him. She said she saw others either join in on the bullying or ignore it because they were too scared to try to stop it.

Before his death, Kenneth's mom remembers that he told her, "Mom, you don't know how it feels to be hated." One commenter on his Facebook memorial site reflects: "I hate to think of what he must have gone through to decide suicide was his only option. I hope and pray all of these bullies feel responsible for what happened." [xxv]

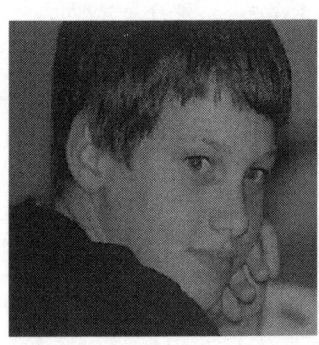

Ryan Halligan, a 13-year-old from Vermont, could see no other way to escape his cyberbullies. He committed suicide in 2003. One boy began a rumor online claiming Ryan was gay. A girl Ryan knew pretended to be interested in him only to ridicule him for believing her. Ryan's story was featured on "Growing Up Online," the PBS documentary.

Ryan told someone he considered an online friend that he was ready to commit suicide and his friend replied: "The last time i hear u complain? ur finally gonna kill urself? Its about (blank)-ing time."

Ryan ended the conversation with, "You'll hear about it in the papers tomorrow."

Ryan's body was found by his sister.[xxvi]

Sexting and how it can backfire

Read
You may not think that forwarding a private picture of someone is bullying, but this could really hurt a person and cause them to be bullied.

The following stories are retold with permission from Puresight.com

Jessica (Jesse) Logan, was a high school senior in Ohio. She committed suicide after she sent a nude photo of herself to her boyfriend that he then sent to everyone at their school after they broke up. The girls at her school harassed Jesse, calling her a "slut" and "whore." Jesse's grades dropped and she started skipping school. At school, she would hide in the bathroom to avoid her bullies.

Jesse told her story on a local television station in 2008, saying: "I just want to make sure no one else will have to go through this again." Just two months after sharing her story on TV, Jesse went to the funeral of a boy who had committed suicide, then went home and committed suicide herself. Jesse's mom found her in her closet.[xxvii]

Hope Witsell was a 13-year-old who forwarded a nude picture of herself to a boy she liked. When another girl borrowed the boy's phone, she found the picture and sent it to other students. Hope's picture was sent to a lot of other students in her school and other schools. Hope's bullies called her a "slut" and "whore."

When school authorities found out about the nude picture near the end of the school year, they suspended Hope for the first week of eighth grade, which started in August.

A counselor noticed cuts on Hope's legs when she returned to school and asked her to sign a "no-harm" contract. In the "no-harm" contract, Hope agreed she would tell an adult if she felt she wanted to hurt herself again.

The day after Hope signed the "no-harm" contract, she committed suicide in her bedroom.[xxviii]

Criminal charges have been filed against many bullies especially if there is physical harm or a suicide involved. The police are able to track cyberbullying back to a computer or smart phone. Once a message or image is out there, it cannot be retrieved, and they can and will find you.

Reflect
Take a good look at each of these pictures and read their stories. Suicide is permanent. They are never coming back. They will never get to experience the joys of getting married, having children and making memories with their family and friends.

These were real people with real feelings and real families.

Suicide was not the answer, speaking up or asking for help is the *ONLY* answer.

Encouragement
What can you do if you have realized you have been bullying someone? It is never too late to start making things right. If you have hurt someone, tell them you're sorry. They may not forgive you, but what matters is that you took a step to atone for your actions. Start doing right and see the wonderful changes that will happen in your life.

People can change
There are celebrities who have admitted they were bullies growing up, including Tina Fey. Famous comedienne Tina Fey admits that she was a mean girl as a child and called it "a disease that had to be conquered." Tina says

she realized later in life why she became a bully—she was using it to help herself feel equal to her peers and as a way of "leveling the playing field." But Tina says her bullying didn't actually level the playing field: "Saying something terrible about someone else does not actually level the playing field."[xxix]

4

Victims

"If you have been brutally broken, but still have the courage to be gentle to other living beings, then you're a bad*** with the heart of an angel."
Keanu Reeves

Learn
It's not always easy to know if you are being bullied. Sometimes, someone's actions can seem mean, but the intent was not to hurt you. Other times, it is clear the intent was to cause you or someone you know harm. Here are some questions you can ask yourself to see if you are a victim of bullying:

- Do other kids ever hit, kick, push or punch me?
- Am I called mean names by other kids?
- Have other kids ever laughed when someone hurt me?
- Has anyone ever made me do something that I didn't want to do?
- Have I not wanted to go to school or ride the bus because I was afraid of another kid?
- Have I ever tried to stop someone from hurting me or harming me, but they just

keep doing it?
- Has anyone ever made fun of me for being good at something?
- Do other kids often tell me that they don't want to play with me?
- Has anyone ever made fun of me for something that I don't do as well as other kids?
- Has anyone ever sent me mean messages?[xxx]

Encouragement

"What makes you different is what makes you beautiful."
Selena Gomez

You are only a victim if you let someone have power over you. You ARE a strong individual that needs to know that bullies do not have power over you. It may be easier said than done, but you can do it!

In the book "The Four Agreements," Don Miguel Ruiz tells us, "Don't Take Things Personally." I know it is easier said than done, but you must put the negative things people say to you out of your head. Take what they said and turn it into strength to make you want to work harder to achieve your dreams and goals.

I know a girl who was in junior high and on a bowling league. Her average was so high that when she went into high school the freshman varsity team wanted her. She joined the league, then her friends started making fun of her. So, what did she do? She quit something she loved because she let others tell her it wasn't the cool thing to be doing.

Finding Your Place
You can help yourself feel empowered by doing these simple things:
- Know that you will not be understood by everyone, and that's okay
- Do things because you love to do them, not because you want to please other people
- Let go of the need to manage other people's perceptions of you
- Surround yourself with people who love you and care about you

"Don't chase people. Be yourself, do your own thing and work hard. The right people—the ones who really belong in your life—will come to you. And stay.
Will Smith

If you enjoy ballet, violin, piano, dancing, cooking, gaming club, playing in the band or anything else and people call you names or tease you for it, ignore them. NEVER let your friends, or anyone else, keep you from doing what you love. Do what is best for you and forget what everyone else thinks or says. You only need to worry about you and only you. It's YOUR life, not theirs.

Friends should NEVER put you down for something you enjoy doing. They should be encouraging you and lifting you up. If they don't, then they really aren't true friends.

When you look in the mirror, say to yourself: *Today might be hard, but I will get through it. One day I will be so powerful that at a school reunion I can tell my bully that I did not let their negative words or actions impact my life or future.*

Withstanding Pressure
Both boys and girls will pressure you into doing things you might be uncomfortable doing, or things that might be illegal. NEVER BE PRESSURED INTO DOING ANYTHING YOU DO NOT WANT TO DO. If you say no, do not let them bully you into changing your mind. Keep your integrity.

Take pride in yourself. You are so special, and you probably don't even realize it. You are a strong individual with a life to live and the passion to share your love with everyone in need.

Read
If you are a victim of bullying, remember that you are not alone. Some of the most famous people

today were bullied when they were younger, and they were able to overcome their bullying to do great things.

Rihanna says she was bullied as a child because her skin was lighter than her classmates, and as she grew older, because she had breasts.[xxxi]

Olympic gold medalist Michael Phelps said he was made fun of in middle school for his big ears and hyper personality.[xxxii]

Lady Gaga says she was teased by her peers. They called her ugly and annoying and said she had a big nose.[xxxiii]

Justin Timberlake says kids called him weird, different and bad names in school. He thanks his mom for teaching him that he could use what people saw as different to make a difference.[xxxiv]

Demi Lovato says that when she was 12, she was bullied so badly she had to become home schooled. She says her peers created a petition for her to commit suicide, and people around the school were signing it.[xxxv]

Encouragement

"This isn't a high school thing or an age thing. It's a people thing. People cut other people down out of jealousy, because of something

broken inside them, or for no reason at all. Just don't let them change you or stop you from singing or dancing around to your favorite song."
Taylor Swift

Do not let a bully defeat you! You have so much to offer. Stand tall and be strong! If you need help, there are plenty of resources that are here waiting and wanting to help you.

Just in case you need to be told today:

You are enough. Your process is perfect for you. You are not ahead of anyone. You are not behind anyone. This journey is your expression of who you were made to be, there is not another person on this Earth that can fulfill that expression.

The Power of Prayer
For those who believe in God or a higher being, keep praying. Pray for guidance, pray for strength, pray for a solution. Sit quietly and listen for the answer. You were not born to be someone's punching bag. Yes, words hurt. But consider where the hurtful words are coming from. They are coming from someone who is hurting, and this is the only way they know how to cope. I'm not making any excuses for them or what they do. I'm just asking you not to let their lives destroy yours.

When you get home and you had a hard day, if you can, pray for those who made your day hard if that is what you believe in. Pray that they can find the good inside themselves. Pray that they will finally realize they are hurting people and doing wrong. Pray that they can find the help they need so they realize that they are victims and they are better than that. It's natural to want your enemy to feel the same type of pain you feel. But that would make you as bad as they are. You are better than that!

Focus on something that you love: writing, music, playing an instrument, painting or anything else that you like. Put your energy towards an activity that makes you feel good. It's okay if you are doing it alone. Once you can find peace within yourself, you will realize that you don't need anyone else.

YOU CAN BE THE DIFFERENCE

5

Bystanders

Read
The following story was written by the boy who became a friend rather than turning his back on a boy being bullied.

A STORY ABOUT A BOY NAMED KYLE[xxxvi]
Reprinted with permission from LifeAdvancer.

One day, when I was a freshman in high school, I saw a kid from my class was walking home from school. His name was Kyle. It looked like he was carrying all of his books. I thought to myself, "Why would anyone bring home all his books on a Friday? He must really be a nerd."

I had quite a weekend planned (parties and a football game with my friends tomorrow afternoon), so I shrugged my shoulders and went on. As I was walking, I saw a bunch of kids running toward him. They ran at him, knocking all his books out of his arms and tripping him so he landed in the dirt. His glasses went flying, and I saw them land in the grass about ten feet from him. He looked up and I saw this terrible sadness in his eyes. My heart went out to him. So, I jogged over to him and as he crawled around looking for his glasses, and I saw a tear in his eye. As I handed him his glasses, I said, "Those guys are jerks. They really should get lives." He looked at me and said, "Hey thanks!"

There was a big smile on his face. It was one of those smiles that showed real gratitude.

I helped him pick up his books, and asked him where he lived. As it turned out, he lived near me, so I asked him why I had never seen him before. He said he had gone to private school before now. I would have never hung out with a private school kid before. We talked all the way home, and I carried some of his books. He turned out to be a pretty cool kid. I asked him if he wanted to play a little football with my friends. He said yes.

We hung out all weekend and the more I got to know Kyle, the more I liked him, and my friends thought the same of him. Monday morning came, and there was Kyle with the huge stack of books again. I stopped him and said, "Boy, you are gonna really build some serious muscles with this pile of books everyday!" He just laughed and handed me half the books.

Over the next four years, Kyle and I became best friends. When we were seniors, we began to think about college. Kyle decided on Georgetown, and I was going to Duke. I knew that we would always be friends, that the miles would never be a problem. He was going to be a doctor, and I was going for business on a football scholarship.

Kyle was valedictorian of our class. I teased him all the time about being a nerd. He had to prepare a speech for graduation. I was so glad it wasn't me having to get up there and speak.

Graduation day, I saw Kyle. He looked great. He was one of those guys that really found himself during high school. He filled out and actually looked good in glasses. He had more dates than I had and all the girls loved him. Boy, sometimes I was jealous. Today was one of those days. I could see that he was nervous about his speech. So, I smacked him on the back and said, "Hey, big guy, you'll be great!" He looked at me with one of those looks (the really grateful one) and smiled. "Thanks," he said.

As he started his speech, he cleared his throat, and began. "Graduation is a time to thank those who helped you make it through those tough years. Your parents, your teachers, your siblings, maybe a coach...but mostly your friends... I am here to tell all of you that being a friend to someone is the best gift you can give them. I am going to tell you a story." I just looked at my friend with disbelief as he told the story of the first day we met.

He had planned to kill himself over the weekend. He talked of how he had cleaned out his locker so his Mom wouldn't have to do it later and was carrying his stuff home. He looked hard at me and gave me a little smile. "Thankfully, I was saved. My friend saved me from doing the unspeakable.. I heard the gasp go through the crowd as this handsome, popular boy told us all about his weakest moment. I saw his Mom and Dad looking at me and smiling that same grateful smile. Not until that moment did I realize it's depth.

Never underestimate the power of your actions. With one small gesture you can change a person's life. For better or for worse. God puts us all in each others lives to impact one another in some way. Look for God in others.

Friends are angels who lift us to our feet when our wings have trouble remembering how to fly.

Reflect

"Knowing what's right doesn't mean much unless you do what's right."
President Theodore Roosevelt

If you are not the bully and not the victim, how would you feel if you saw someone being bullied and did nothing? How would you feel if you were the one who pushed him down?

Encouragement

"I've realized that you become a bully if you are just watching someone get bullied and you don't say anything. Speak up!"
Emma Roberts

Sometimes watching someone being bullied can be just as frightening as being the victim. Bystanders are people like friends, other students, peers, teachers, parents, and coaches who witness bullying but do not do anything to stop it. Often, bystanders who witness bullying find it upsetting and are afraid to stop the bullying or report it because the bully could come after them.[xxxvii]

So, what do you do if you see someone being bullied? You can make a big difference by stopping the bullying as it is happening or reporting the bullying to a trusted adult. Don't be afraid to stand up to the bully on behalf of the victim. By standing up for a victim, you have made a lasting impression on them. They will always remember you for what you have done. By helping, you are letting them know that they are not alone and that someone cares. You are showing them that someone has their back. If you see something, say something.

> *"What hurts the victim most is not the cruelty of the oppressor, but the silence of the bystander."*
> Elie Wiesel

6

I PLEDGE TO BE AN UPSTANDER

Reprinted with permission from the Tyler Clementi Foundation.

I pledge to be an Upstander:

I will stand up to bullying whether I'm at school, at home, at work, in my house of worship, whether I am speaking in the digital cyber world or out in the real world with friends, family, colleagues or teammates.

I will work to make others feel safe and included by treating them with kindness, respect and compassion.

I will not use insulting or demeaning language, slurs, gestures, facial expressions, or jokes about anyone's sexuality, size, gender, race, any kind of disability, religion, class, politics, or other differences, in person or while using technology.

If I realize I have hurt someone I will apologize.

I will remain vigilant and not be a passive audience or "bystander" to abusive actions or words.

If I see or hear behavior that perpetuates prejudice:

I will speak up! I will let others know that bullying, cruelty, and prejudice are abusive and not acceptable.

If I do not feel safe or if my intervention does not change the poor behaviors, I will tell a trusted adult or person of authority.

I will reach out to someone I know who has been the target of abusive actions or words and let this person know that this is not okay with me and ask how I can help.

If I learn in person or online that someone is feeling seriously depressed or potentially suicidal:

I will reach out and tell this person, "Your life has value and is important, no matter how you feel at the moment, and no matter what others say or think."

I will strongly encourage this person to get professional help.[xxxviii]

7

MAKE A DIFFERENCE

*"Strong people stand up for themselves.
But....the strongest people stand up for others."
Chris Gardner*

Encouragement
The best thing you can do is try to make a difference and build up the people around you.

If you see someone who has been left out or sitting alone, ask them to join you.
If you see someone crying, ask if there is anything you can do.
If you see someone who was pushed down, help them up.
If you see someone being bullied, stand up for them.
If you see someone sitting on the side lines, ask them if they want to play.

You can also be on the lookout for peers who look like they may be struggling. Here are some warning signs you might see if a friend, loved one or classmate is thinking about committing suicide.

Suicide warning signs or suicidal thoughts include, but are not limited to:

- Talking about suicide or telling a friend or family member "I'm going to kill myself," "I wish I were dead" or "I wish I hadn't been born"
- Buying a gun, saving pills or keeping another weapon to harm oneself
- Withdrawing from friends and other activities and wanting to be alone
- Having a deep interest in death, dying or violence
- Feeling trapped, hopeless or overwhelmed about a situation you can't seem to fix
- Changing your normal routine, such as eating less or sleeping more than usual
- Saying goodbye to people as if you won't see them again
- Changing your personality or feeling very anxious or agitated, especially when you are experiencing the other warning signs of suicide or suicidal thoughts

The warning signs for suicide aren't always obvious, and they can be different depending on the person.

If you're feeling suicidal, but you aren't thinking of hurting yourself right now, your best option is to reach out for help.

- Talk to a close friend or family member about how you are feeling
- Talk to a trusted adult like a pastor/rabbi, youth group leader, teacher, coach or counselor
- Call a suicide hotline (see below)
- Go to the doctor or a mental health professional

If you think you may attempt suicide, you should get help immediately!

- Call 911
- Call the National Suicide Prevention Lifeline at 1-800-273-TALK (1-800-273-8255) any time of day.
- Text HELP to 741741 any time of day for anonymous, free crisis counseling.[xxxix]

8

RESOURCES

A Trusted Adult: Your first line of defense should be to find an adult you can trust and report any bullying or abuse you experience or see. This can be a teacher, principal, counselor, parent, pastor/priest/rabbi, youth group leader or other adult you trust.

B.A.C.A. Bikers Against Child Abuse: If you are afraid to walk to school because of bullying, these bikers (if they can) will give you a ride to school on their motorcycles. Once the bullies see you on a motorcycle with a group of bikers, they may back down. If they don't, the bikers will stay with you until they do. http://bacaworld.org.

LGBTQ+ Resources and Help Lines: The Trevor Project (866-488-7386) & The Trans Lifeline (877-565-8860)

The Jed Foundation 1-800-273-TALK (8255)

Learn more about bullying and the effects it can have on a friend and their family. You can also learn more about what you can do if you see or experience bullying:

- Stopbullying.gov

- TeensAgainstBullying.org
- KidsAgainstBullying.org

Books:

- 13 Reasons Why, by Jay Asher
- The Chocolate War, by Robert Cormier
- Dear Bully: Seventy Authors Tell Their Stories, by Megan Kelley and Carrie Jones
- It Gets Better: Coming Out, Overcoming Bullying, and Creating a Life Worth Living, edited by Dan Savage and Terry Miller

Movies:

- A Walk to Remember
- The Kid Who Would be King
- The Karate Kid
- BULLY

9

NEED SOME INSPIRATION?

"A smile is definitely a window into someone's soul not only the eyes."
Shakira

"Beauty is only skin deep. I think what's really important is finding a balance of mind, body and spirit."
Jennifer Lopez

"To be a champ, you have to believe in yourself when no one else will."
Sugar Ray Robinson

"I would rather be a little nobody than to be an evil somebody."
President Abraham Lincoln

"I am a true believer in karma. You get what you give, whether it's bad or good."
Sandra Bullock

"If they don't like you for being yourself, be yourself even more."
Taylor Swift

*"Your imperfections make you beautiful, they make you who you are.
So just be yourself, love yourself for who you are and just keep going."*
Demi Lovato

"Don't ever let a soul in the world tell you that you can't be exactly who you are."
Lady Gaga

"Being yourself is all it takes. If you want to impress someone don't be someone else just be yourself."
Selena Gomez

"Your self-worth is determined by you. You don't have to depend on someone telling you who you are."
Beyoncé

"I was bullied every second of every day in Elementary and Middle School. Obviously, people are going to bring you down because of your drive. But, ultimately, it makes you a stronger person to turn your cheek and go the other way."
Selena Gomez

"Let them judge you. Let them misunderstand you. Let them gossip about you. Their opinions aren't your problem. You stay kind, committed to love, and free in your authenticity. No matter what they do or say don't you dare doubt your

worth or the beauty of your truth. Just keep on shining like you do."
Scott Stable

"Your time is limited, so don't waste it living someone else's life. Don't be trapped by dogma—which is living with the results of other people's thinking. Don't let the noise of others' opinion drown out your own inner voice. And, most important, have the courage to follow your heart and intuition."
Steve Jobs

"LEARN HOW TO:
Have fun without drinking.
Talk without a phone.
Dream without drugs.
Smile without selfies.
Love without conditions."
Author Unknown

10

ACTIVITY

Do you consider yourself a: _____

    a. Bully
    b. Victim
    c. Bystander
    d. Other

Why?

_____
_____

If you see someone being bullied, would you: _____

    a. Intervene
    b. Do nothing
    c. Record it for social media
    d. Tell a trusted adult

Why?

_____
_____

If you are with a group of people that are using drugs, would you: _____

    a. Try drugs to fit in
    b. Walk away

      c. Try and explain how dangerous it is
      d. Report them

Why?

_____

_____

If you feel like you are a bully, victim, or bystander, what are you going to do about it?

YOU CAN BE THE DIFFERENCE

About the Author

Losing my husband in 2002 left me with two children to raise. It was a difficult time. Having no family support in helping with Jason, I did the best that I could. There were so many challenges with him. But being bullied was one of the hardest things we had to encounter. It was the beginning of most of his troubles.

My whole life I have had zero tolerance towards bullying. I felt helpless because I didn't know what to do when I saw it when I was younger. Now I know and want to encourage others to stand up against bullying and for the victims.

My late husband and I adopted Jason when I found out I couldn't have children of our own. He was 21 months old. He was a beautiful, happy and spunky child. He was always trying to please everyone.

Jason always knew that he was adopted. When he was five, Jason was playing with the neighbor boy and told him he was adopted. The boy went home and asked his mother what adopted meant and she said that it is when the mother doesn't want the kid. She said this in front of Jason. This is a perfect example of how words can impact a person and how it is best to *THINK* before you speak. Words hurt.

Jason would think about his birth mother a lot

and would ask, "why didn't she want me?" and "what was wrong with me?" because of what his friend's mother said. No matter what I told him and how much I encouraged him, he could not accept the answer. I tried telling him that she loved him so much that she wanted him to have a better life than what she could give him.

As he grew older, kids began to tease him for being a husky child. He tried so hard to make friends but just couldn't seem to find anyone who wanted to be a good friend to him.

In junior high, the bullying really started to escalate. Children called him fat, stupid, and ugly. For a child who just wanted to be accepted, this was devastating to Jason and he couldn't understand why everyone had to be so cruel.

As he faced bullying at school, he began to lose his self-confidence. He tried desperately to get people to like and want him.

To numb the pain, Jason started doing drugs. The bullying continued and so did the drug abuse. He was addicted before high school. He hid this very well from us. The drugs began to damage his brain. He became very paranoid, psychotic, began hearing voices, and lost touch with reality. One of the medications the doctors had put him on for these issues made him gain a lot of weight. This was no life, and for no reason other than the bullying. Do I miss him?

Of course I do, every day. But knowing that he is not suffering anymore gives me some peace.

To watch a child suffer the way Jason did was unbearable. My daughter and I tried everything we could to let him know how much he was loved. But it wasn't enough.

I had to kick him out of the house for his stealing and drug abuse. He had threatened me and my daughter and I did not feel safe anymore. He was homeless for a while and enjoyed being out of the house. Jason's death turned my life upside down. I then became the target of bullying from ex-family members who told me I should be embarrassed and ashamed of myself, that a real mother should always be there for her kids. Yet no one knew what I had gone through because there was not one family member who cared enough to ask. They only assumed the worst of me. They judged me before finding out the facts. Another form of bullying. I have forgiven them in my heart so I can live in peace and I chose not to have them in my life anymore.

I had kicked him out and taken him back so many times and nothing ever changed. I gave him every opportunity I could think of to help him get clean from drugs and live a better life.

Why is this book so important to me? Unless you have lived with a person who was constantly bullied, you will never understand. It has become my mission to spread the word about bullying. To help others take a good look at themselves and their words and actions. To help them be the difference.

REFERENCES

[i] "11 Facts About Bullying." *DoSomething.org.* https://www.dosomething.org/us/facts/11-facts-about-bullying. Accessed 31 January 2020.

[ii] "Bullying and Suicide." *Bullying Statistics Organization.* http://www.bullyingstatistics.org/content/bullying-and-suicide.html. Accessed 31 January 2020.

[iii] Narcisco, Dean. "Family, community struggles for answers after 11-year-old fatally shoots herself." *The Columbus Dispatch.* Oct. 29, 2016. https://www.dispatch.com/content/stories/local/2016/10/29/family-community-struggles-for-answers-after-11-year-old-fatally-shoots-herself.html

[iv] "11 Facts About Bullying." *DoSomething.org.* https://www.dosomething.org/us/facts/11-facts-about-bullying. Accessed 31 January 2020.

[v] "Facts About Bullying." *Stopbullying.gov.* www.stopbullying.gov/resources/facts. Accessed 31 January 2020.

[vi] "Effects of Bullying." *Stopbullying.gov.* www.stopbullying.gov/bullying/effects. Accessed 31 January 2020.

[vii] "Sexting." *Miriam Webster Dictionary.* https://www.merriam-webster.com/dictionary/sexting. Accessed 31 January 2020.

[viii] "Facts on Bullying." *Bullyingstatistics.org.* http://www.bullyingstatistics.org/content/facts-on-bullying.html. Accessed 31 January 2020.

[ix] "Facts on Bullying." *Bullyingstatistics.org.* http://www.bullyingstatistics.org/content/facts-on-bullying.html. Accessed 31 January 2020.

[x] "Who Is at Risk." *Stopbullying.gov.* https://www.stopbullying.gov/bullying/at-risk. Accessed 31 January 2020.

[xi] "Effects of Bullying." *Stopbullying.gov.*

www.stopbullying.gov/bullying/effects. Accessed 31 January 2020.

[xii] "The 1 of 4 Middle School Bullies Decides to Apologize After 11 Years." Reprinted with permission from *The Bully Project.* http://www.thebullyproject.com/the_1_of_4_middle_school_bullies_decides_to_apologize_after_11_years. Accessed 31 January 2020.

[xiii] "Friendships: Enrich Your Life and Improve Your Health." *Mayo Clinic.* www.mayoclinic.org/health-lifestyle/adult-health/in-depth/friendships/art-20044860. Accessed 31 January 2020.

[xiv] "The Long Term Effects of Bullying." *Mental Help Net.* https://www.mentalhelp.net/abuse/long-term-effects-of-bullying/. Accessed 31 January 2020.

[xv] Gordon, Sherri. "6 Ways Bullying Impacts the Family." *Very Well Family.* January 20, 2020. https://www.verywellfamily.com/how-bullying-impacts-the-family-460805

[xvi] "Effects of Bullying." *Stopbullying.gov.* www.stopbullying.gov/bullying/effects. Accessed 31 January 2020.

[xvii] Hobson, Elton. "High school football team lets water boy with special needs score touchdown to surprise terminally ill mom." *Global News.* Sept. 20, 2016. https://globalnews.ca/news/2951943/high-school-football-team-lets-water-boy-with-special-needs-score-touchdown-to-surprise-terminally-ill-mom/

[xviii] Hartman, Steve. "Mich. Middle school football team conspires for touching touchdown. *CBS News.* Oct. 26, 2013. https://www.cbsnews.com/news/mich-middle-school-football-team-conspires-for-touching-touchdown/

[xix] Zajac, Kirk. "One Teen was Bullied to Suicide. A Bullying Story, From The Bully." Reprinted with permission from *Your Teen Mag.* https://yourteenmag.com/social-life/teen-bullying-tips/suicide-one-teens-bullying-story. Accessed 31 January 2020.

[xx] "Tyler Clementi's Story." Retold with permission from *Tyler Clementi Foundation.* https://tylerclementi.org/tylers-story/. Accessed 31 January 2020.

[xxi] "Hannah Smith 1999-2013." Retold with permission from *Pure Sight Online Child Safety.* https://puresight.com/Real-Life-Stories/hannah-smith.html. Accessed 31 January 2020.
[xxii] "Phoebe Prince." Retold with permission from *Pure Sight Online Child Safety.* https://puresight.com/Real-Life-Stories/phoebe-prince.html. Accessed 31 January 2020.
[xxiii] Webley, Kayla. "Teens Who Admitted to Bullying Phoebe Prince Sentenced." *Time Magazine.* May 5, 2011. https://newsfeed.time.com/2011/05/05/teens-who-admitted-to-bullying-phoebe-prince-sentenced/
[xxiv] "David Molak 2000-2016." Retold with permission from *Pure Sight Online Child Safety.* https://puresight.com/Real-Life-Stories/david-molak-2000-2016-puresight.html. Accessed 31 January 2020.
[xxv] "Kenneth Weishuhn (14)." Retold with permission from *Lead Them Home. Loving LGBT+ People in the Church.* https://www.leadthemhome.org/2012/10/kenneth-weishuhn-14.html#.Xi98jC3Mx24. Accessed 31 January 2020.
[xxvi] "Ryan Halligan: A Bullying Casualty." Retold with permission from *Lead Them Home. Loving LGBT+ People in the Church.* https://www.leadthemhome.org/2010/11/ryan-halligan-bullying-casualty.html#.Xi99Ui3Mx24. Accessed 31 January 2020.
[xxvii] "Jessica Logan 1990-2008." Retold with permission from *Pure Sight Online Child Safety.* https://puresight.com/Real-Life-Stories/jessica-logan-1990-2008.html. Accessed 31 January 2020.
[xxviii] "Hope Witsell." Retold with permission from *Pure Sight Online Child Safety.* https://puresight.com/Real-Life-Stories/hope-witsell.html. Accessed 31 January 2020.
[xxix] McKenzie, Joi-Marie. "Tina Fey Admits She Was a 'Mean Girl' in High School." *ABCNews.com.* Dec. 19, 2015. https://abcnews.go.com/Entertainment/tina-fey-admits-girl-high-school/story?id=35861388
[xxx] "Are You A Target of Bullying?" *PACERKidsAgainstBullying.org.* https://pacerkidsagainstbullying.org/are-you-a-target/. Accessed 31 January 2020.
[xxxi] Abadi, Mark. "9 Wildly Successful People Who Were Bullied as Kids." *Business Insider.* Dec. 11, 2017.

https://www.businessinsider.com/successful-people-who-were-bullied-2017-12

[xxxii] Abadi, Mark. "9 Wildly Successful People Who Were Bullied as Kids." *Business Insider.* Dec. 11, 2017. https://www.businessinsider.com/successful-people-who-were-bullied-2017-12

[xxxiii] Abadi, Mark. "9 Wildly Successful People Who Were Bullied as Kids." *Business Insider.* Dec. 11, 2017. https://www.businessinsider.com/successful-people-who-were-bullied-2017-12

[xxxiv] Abadi, Mark. "9 Wildly Successful People Who Were Bullied as Kids." *Business Insider.* Dec. 11, 2017. https://www.businessinsider.com/successful-people-who-were-bullied-2017-12

[xxxv] Dzhanova, Yelena. "Demi Lovato's Latest Hit Song is Dedicated to Her Childhood Bullies." *NBCNews.com.* Sept. 24, 2017. https://www.nbcnews.com/news/us-news/demi-lovato-s-latest-hit-song-dedicated-her-childhood-bullies-n804341

[xxxvi] Walden, Holly. "This Touching Story about a Bullied Boy Shows How a Small Gesture Can Save Someone's Life." Reprinted with permission from *Life Advancer*. 27 December 2016. https://www.lifeadvancer.com/touching-story-bullied-boy/

[xxxvii] "Bystanders to Bullying." *Stopbullying.gov.* www.stopbullying.gov/prevention/bystanders-to-bullying. Accessed 31 January 2020.

[xxxviii] "Join the Million Upstander." Reprinted with permission from *Tyler Clementi Foundation.* https://tylerclementi.org/pledge/. Accessed 31 January 2020.

[xxxix] "Suicide and Suicidal Thoughts." *Mayo Clinic.* https://www.mayoclinic.org/diseases-conditions/suicide/symptoms-causes/syc-20378048. Accessed 31 January 2020.